D0791965

T1-BJR-619

TABLE OF CONTENTS

WHAT IS A DIGITAL FOOTPRINT?

Every time you use the Internet, you leave a little bit of your personal information behind. This trail is called your digital footprint. It is as if you are walking on a trail and leaving breadcrumbs behind. Each breadcrumb represents a digital footprint. Each breadcrumb is small. But together, they form an entire loaf of bread. Likewise, your individual digital footprints are linked. They form an entire profile—all about you!

Your digital footprint contains pieces of information. It may include your name, address, phone number, and birthday. It also contains things you upload and actions you take. You are always leaving digital footprints, even if they are not visible. As you use the Internet, your activity is tracked and recorded. These records add only a tiny bit of information to your entire digital footprint. Your digital footprint grows larger in a very short amount of time. Each newly loaded website, "Like" on Facebook, and e-mail draft are recorded and remembered forever.

Every button you hit online adds to your digital footprint.

How many websites do you think you visit in a day? Now that you have thought about it, is the number higher than you expected? How might the number of sites you visit contribute to your digital footprint?

3.1 billion

Approximate number of global Internet users in March 2015.

- Your Internet activity is tracked and recorded.
- As Internet use increases, digital footprints grow larger.
- Hundreds of pieces of data contribute to a person's digital footprint.

Imagine shopping online for a new pair of jeans. First, you land on the store's homepage. By clicking on the "jeans" tab, you are taken to a new webpage. Clicking an image to view more details opens another page. Each action you take is traced and recorded. Those actions are part of your digital footprint.

The more you use the Internet, the larger your digital footprint grows. Your digital footprint is not a bad thing or a good thing. But learning about your digital footprint can help you understand what happens to your information online. It can help you see why it is important to be careful about what you share. Knowing how your digital footprint works keeps you safer online.

Shopping online leaves digital breadcrumbs behind.

ONLINE·SHOP

DOES MY INFORMATION STAY ONLINE FOREVER?

Have you ever created an account on a website? You might have entered your first and last name. You probably had to provide an e-mail address. People enter a lot of personal information on websites. But many people do not think about what happens with that information.

E-mail, chat, and social media allow you to share your interests and talents. You may think only friends and family can see what you share and write. You may also think that deleting information makes it go away forever. But information you share over e-mail and social media never truly goes away. It often can be seen by many others. Future employers, college recruiters,

College recruiters might search your name online.

ADMISSIONS

Taking selfies is fun, but think before you share one online.

business clients, and teachers may be able to find it. It is viewable even if it is years old. The information might not be bad. But who you are in the future may be different from who you are today.

What you post on the Internet can be seen by anyone who follows you. This is especially true for mobile applications such as Instagram and Snapchat. You may also be sharing your exact location. Check the location settings on your device to see what you are sharing.

76

Percent of social media users between the ages of 9 and 16 who have their Facebook pages set to private.

- Many Internet users do not know how their personal information is used online.
- Things you posted on the Internet in the past can still be seen in the future.
- You could be sharing your exact location, so check the location settings on your device.

HOW DO WEBSITES KNOW WHERE I AM?

Your house, the grocery store, and your school all have street addresses. The Internet network you use also has an address. An Internet company assigns each network an Internet Protocol (IP) address. Imagine you and your family members each use a different computer while at home. Each of your computers is connected to the same Internet network. That network has an IP address. It is unique to your house. Your school has its own IP address. At school, you connect to the Internet through the school's IP address.

IP addresses share small bits of information with websites. It may tell websites your family's name or your school's name. It could share your phone number or your physical location. It may also share a record of your personal Internet activity. Websites use this information to change how they interact with you. Imagine you go online to find the nearest sporting goods store. The

Your school has its own IP address.

store's website may use your location to give you more accurate results.

Your smartphone can also share your location over the Internet. Your phone uses its global positioning system (GPS) to find you. It connects your phone with a nearby cell phone tower. The tower can now track your exact location. But your location is shared over your data network, too. It is possible for people to hack the network and learn your location. Unless you need to use it, keep the location tracker off. Ask an adult to show you how.

Your smartphone can track your location.

Address:
23456
Springtime Square

Phone:
555 546 9867

4:59 PM

address   search

1.6 billion
Number of IP addresses in the United States in 2015.

- Each Internet network has its own IP address.
- Websites can find a user's personal information based on an IP address.
- Your smartphone's map feature shares your location with cell phone towers.

FIND MY FRIENDS

Find My Friends is a mobile application. It accesses your contacts and your smartphone's map feature. You can connect with friends and family on the app. When you share your location, an alert becomes visible to your family and friends. Friends who use the app also show up on the map.

9

HOW DO WEBSITES USE COOKIES?

Your digital footprint is made up of bits of data. Every time you visit a website, you leave a bit behind. Websites collect these bits of data. They use them to learn more about you.

A website links all of your bits of data together using a cookie. A cookie strings together the actions you take. It tracks when you click on a button or enter your username. It packages the information into one long strand. It adds the cookie to a file in your computer's browser. When you visit the same website again, it finds the cookie. This helps the site recognize you and your personal settings. You will not have to provide the same information each time you visit a site. Some

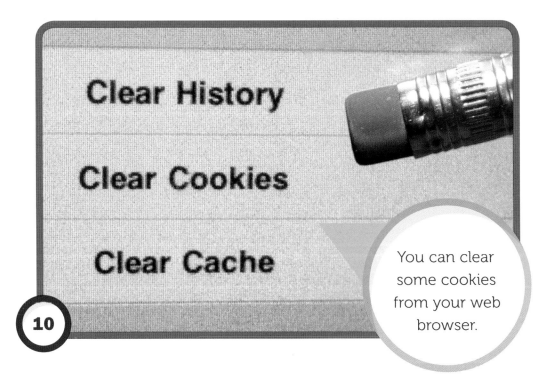

Clear History

Clear Cookies

Clear Cache

You can clear some cookies from your web browser.

cookies are deleted once you close your browser. Others are kept until you delete them. Ask an adult to help you learn how.

The cookie helps a website remember your personal information. But it also records your every visit. For every new website you visit, another cookie is added to the browser file. Most browsers store thousands of cookies. That is why cookies are one of the biggest contributors to your growing footprint.

34

Average number of cookies a website stores in your browser on your first visit.

- A website links all of your actions together using a cookie.
- A cookie keeps a record of each time you visit a website.
- Cookies are one of the biggest contributors to your digital footprint.

Web browsers store cookies from websites you use.

DOES MY DIGITAL SHADOW FOLLOW ME?

Everyone who uses the Internet has a digital footprint. But it is possible to find information online about people who have never used the Internet. The things others upload about you make up your digital shadow. They include digital medical records, bank records, and even criminal history reports.

Much of your personal information is visible to anyone who looks for it. Someone can search for you online using a search engine. They may find photos you have shared on social media. Videos of school concerts or

Your friends may share photos of you online.

1 trillion

Minimum number of Google searches performed every year.

- The information others upload about you on the Internet is called a digital shadow.
- People learn information about you by searching your name in a search engine.
- Google is the most-used search engine in the world.

plays you have been in may show up. So may school newspaper articles that mention your name.

Try typing your own name into a search engine, such as Google. It will show quite a few results. But it shows only small parts of your digital footprint. It will also show you information about others who have the same name. Other websites, such as pipl.com, can find information not included on regular search engines. Try your search while you are on a different Internet network. If you search from home, Google already knows you are the user. It may use your IP address to show you results based on your location.

You can search for yourself online.

Social media

HOW DO COMPANIES USE DIGITAL FOOTPRINTS?

The information in your digital footprint creates a virtual profile of you. Companies use this information to try to sell you products, goods, or services. Three different kinds of website companies work together to gather information about Internet users.

Imagine you create an account on your favorite game website. You provide your name, e-mail address, and age. You may even share where you live. The website creates two cookies. One cookie is for your web browser. It will remember your information the next time you sign in. The other cookie is for an aggregator. An aggregator is a type of website company. It collects information about different users from websites. Aggregators collect information from many different users. It sorts them into categories. Then it sells that information to another type of company, a publisher.

Now imagine you create an account on a new gaming website. You

Game apps may have ads.

http://storify.com/

Storify by livefy

Make the web tell a

1

> Storify puts your social media posts into a single profile.

share the same information with this site. After you sign in, you notice an ad for a game you might like. The ad was created by the publisher. In this case, the publisher is the gaming website. It bought data about you from the aggregator. The publisher and aggregator knew you might like the game in the ad. The company that sells the game is called the advertiser. The advertiser buys ads from the publisher. It hopes you will buy the game.

1

Number of websites in the 100 most-visited websites completely free of advertisements.

- Aggregators, publishers, and advertisers work together to gather information about Internet users.
- Advertisers and publishers often work together to place an advertisement online.
- The companies use your information to create ads for products you might buy.

STORIFY

Storify is an online aggregator. Storify asks users to sign into their social media profiles. It pulls information from their profiles into a single story. It gives users a big picture view of everything they have shared on social media.

WILL MY ONLINE IMAGE TODAY AFFECT MY FUTURE?

Suppose you want to run for public office someday or own your own business. The way you manage your online image today will likely affect your future opportunities.

To run for public office, you will likely need a college degree. Many colleges look at a student's digital footprint before accepting them. Colleges want to know their students are responsible inside and outside of the classroom. Social media can show what kind of person you are. A school may look there first.

Your online interactions with other people also contribute to your online reputation. Your friends can see comments you leave on their social media pages. But unless you change your privacy settings, so can all of your friends' contacts. Anyone can see your comments on a

Colleges may look at your digital footprint.

be – Broadcast Yourself.

/youtube.com/

You Tube

Join the largest worldwide video-shar

YouTube comments can be seen by anyone.

YouTube video or other website. If you start a fight or bully someone online, those comments could become public. Lawyers have even used online comments as evidence in court cases.

WATCH OUT FOR VIRAL PHOTOS AND VIDEOS

Viral videos and photos can put your future at risk. When a video or photo goes viral, it is shared all over the Internet. It is seen by thousands and sometimes millions of people. If a negative photo or video of you goes viral, it may affect your chances of getting into your favorite college. It could also make it difficult to find a job once you are done with school.

31

Percent of college admissions officers in 2013 who used social media to learn more about an applicant.

- Some colleges look at the social media pages of their applicants.
- Comments made on news, entertainment, and other sites are public.
- Lawyers have used public social media posts as evidence in court cases.

CAN MY DIGITAL FOOTPRINT PUT ME AT RISK?

Companies track what you do on the Internet. But if some companies find your personal information, it could be used for more than advertising purposes. For example, some company websites allow you to download music, films, or TV shows illegally. Visiting these sites can put you at risk. Files you download could contain viruses that attack your computer. Or, a company could send a virus to your e-mail address.

An e-mail virus is sent to your inbox just like a regular message. It may look like it is sent from a person. But if you do not recognize the name, do not open it. An e-mail virus may be attached. If the file is downloaded and opened, the virus will infect your computer. Files with an EXE or VBS extension commonly contain viruses.

Protect yourself and never open attachments from people you do not know.

SPOTIFY

Spotify is a website that lets you enjoy music legally. Spotify users do not download music. Instead, they stream it online. They can listen, but no file is downloaded to their computers. Using streaming services such as Spotify can help you avoid downloading viruses.

Anything you download from the Internet becomes part of your digital footprint. You can protect yourself by not visiting sites that offer illegal downloading. Instead, find sites that stream music and video. You may need to pay for these sites. But using legal sites will help you avoid downloading a virus. It will protect you from sharing your e-mail address with an untrustworthy company. It also makes sure you are acting within the law, too.

66

Percent of children ages 12 to 15 who download music.

- An e-mail virus might look like it was sent by a person, just like any other e-mail.
- Files with an EXE or VBS extension are the most notable for containing viruses.
- Illegally downloading music, movies, or TV shows can get you in trouble.

Stream music instead of downloading it illegally.

CAN I DELETE MY DIGITAL FOOTPRINT?

There is no way to actually delete your digital footprint. But you can manage your footprint so the information will not hurt you in the future. Sign into your accounts on the websites you visit. Adjust your privacy settings on these sites. The only things that should be visible to the public are your first name and your current profile picture. Social media websites have step-by-step guides to help you.

Next, make sure you do not offer too much information online. It can be easy to over share on social media sites and other public websites. Do not share your usernames and passwords with strangers or your friends. They may use

your information to harm you. But do share your usernames and passwords with a parent or trusted adult. They can help you stay safe online.

Another powerful way to manage your digital footprint is to clear your cookies. Without cookies, websites cannot remember information about

Only share your passwords with trusted adults.

Congress updated COPPA in 2012.

you. Every web browser has a different process for clearing cookies. Find out how your browser works.

COPPA

Congress put the Children's Online Privacy Protection Act (COPPA) into law in 1998. A new rule took effect in 2013. It gives parents control over what information is collected from their children. This applies to people who are under 13 years old. That is why websites, including Facebook and Snapchat, do not allow users under 13 to create accounts.

86

Percent of Internet users who have taken steps, such as clearing cookies, to remove or mask their digital footprints.

- Make only your first name and a non-revealing profile picture public online.
- Websites have step-by-step guides to help users adjust their privacy settings.
- Never share your home address or where you go to school online.

HOW IS MY DIGITAL FOOTPRINT HELPFUL?

Your digital footprint can be useful. It can be helpful if your identity is stolen. Identity thieves steal personal information. They use the information to get money. Your digital footprint makes it easier to find who stole it and how. Authorities use cookies and location trackers to track down the thief.

Your smartphone can help you track down a thief.

Data on your smartphone apps is also useful. Apps that track your phone's location can help you find your phone if you lose it. Most can pick up a signal from a smartphone even if it is shut off. Ask an adult to help you download one.

Often, cookies are handier than they are hazardous. Imagine you are writing a book report. You need to do some research online. Cookies help your web browser remember websites you have visited. They allow you to access these sites more quickly.

Advertisers and aggregators can be helpful, too. Imagine you just finished a book by a certain author. You share that you enjoyed the book on social media. Aggregators find the information you shared. Eventually, advertisements for useful information about the author will appear as you visit other sites. You may learn about the author's next new book through these ads.

11

CAN MY DIGITAL FOOTPRINT BE POSITIVE?

A digital footprint can seem scary. But your digital footprint can be positive, too. It has the potential to serve you well in the future.

If you use websites as tools for education, your digital footprint can be useful. It will help websites remember you for your next visit. Your digital footprint can make doing research easier. You can use the Internet for a lot of great things.

Your digital footprint can help with homework.

You may meet other students who are interested in learning. Or, you might showcase your talents and creativity. Share images of a project you've been working on. You can even join groups that support a good cause. When you do this, your digital footprint starts to show off your good work. It helps build a positive online reputation.

Try doing extra research on a topic you covered in class. Share what you have learned with your friends on a social media website. Have you taken any artistic photos lately? Add your name to the image to show they are your work. Then, upload those to your social media site rather than photos of you and your friends. You will build a digital footprint that shows who you are without sharing too much personal information.

Your digital footprints will lead you to new opportunities, connections, and ideas. You control the quality of those opportunities. They are based on the quality of the footprints you leave behind.

75

Estimated percent of companies in 2012 that looked at applicants' online reputations before hiring them.

- Your digital footprint can be used to your advantage.
- Share topics you learn in school with your friends on social media sites.
- The quality of the footprints you leave is based on the quality of content you view and post.

Your digital footprint can have a positive effect on your life.

WILL MY DIGITAL FOOTPRINT CHANGE IN THE FUTURE?

Think of your personal information as a type of money. Every day, you trade some of your personal information with different websites.

Signing up for an e-mail address costs you information. You must trade your name, phone number, and other information to get the address.

But you do not always have control over how your information is shared. Others may share your information. And you do not get something in return for them sharing it. This may change in the future. Experts are figuring out ways to give you control of your personal information. Companies will have a harder time gathering your personal information in the future. They may start

What would you want in return for your personal information?

You and your friends' digital footprints may change in the future.

to trade their services for your personal information.

An increase in online privacy may bring about another change. You might notice more educational commercials or advertisements. They will educate the public on how to strengthen their online privacy. This will help people understand how to manage their digital footprints. Their digital footprints will begin to change.

70

Percent of people who believe individuals should own their digital footprints and decide how their personal information is used.

- Experts are coming up with ways to put you in control of your personal information.
- Advertisements may educate the public on how to protect their digital footprints.
- Companies may have a harder time gathering your personal information.

27

FACT SHEET

- There is a good chance that someone will look you up online. College recruiters use the Internet to learn more about applicants. Employers research job candidates, and landlords look up their renters. A family member or friend may want to learn more about you.

- Type your full name into a search engine. If you do not find the right information, try an advanced search. If you do not like what you find, try to see who posted it. If a friend posted it, ask them to remove it. Otherwise, you can contact the site administrator to remove it.

- Use different passwords for each of your usernames. Be sure to change your passwords often. If someone did get a hold of your information, they could not access it without the new password.

- The most important thing you can do to make sure your digital footprint is kept private is to think before you post. Before you put anything online, ask yourself if the content is something you want others to associate with you.

GLOSSARY

advertiser
A company selling a certain product to the public.

aggregator
A website that gathers many pieces of information from around the Internet and keeps it in one place.

cookie
A small amount of online data saved by your web browser.

digital shadow
When personal data is collected or posted without knowledge or consent of the user.

e-mail virus
A computer code sent to you as an e-mail note attachment that, if opened, will cause some unexpected and usually harmful effect.

global positioning system (GPS)
A satellite navigation system used to determine ground position, location, speed, and direction.

hack
To gain access to a computer, smartphone, or tablet illegally.

Internet Protocol (IP) address
A code a computer, smartphone, or tablet needs to access the Internet.

online reputation
How others think of you when they find you online.

publisher
A company that puts up an advertisement on the Internet so that it is visible to the public.

web browser
An application used to access and view websites, such as Google Chrome or Internet Explorer.

FOR MORE INFORMATION

Books

Bennett, Ruth. *Tips for Good Social Networking.* New York: Gareth Stevens Publishing, 2014.

Cindrich, Sharon. *The Smart Girl's Guide to the Internet: How to Connect with Friends, Find What You Need, and Stay Safe Online.* Middleton, WI: American Girl, 2009.

Ohler, Jason B. *Digital Community, Digital Citizen.* Thousand Oaks, CA: Corwin, 2010.

Websites

Federal Trade Commission: Security Plaza
www.consumer.ftc.gov/sites/default/files/games/off-site/youarehere/pages/htmlsite/security_plaza.html

Media Smarts: How Cyber-Savvy Are You?
www.mediasmarts.ca/sites/mediasmarts/files/games/cyber-security-quiz/index_en.html

PBS Kids: Cyberchase
www.pbskids.org/cyberchase

INDEX

About the Author

Jill Roesler was a professional journalist before she began writing children's books. She enjoys doing research and writing about historical topics as well as modern day society. Jill is from Minnesota.